THE QUEST FOR FUEL

We use fuel in all sorts of ways. Our houses, schools, swimming pools and cinemas are kept warm and light with fuel. The chemicals in oil, gas and coal go to make our carpets, our clothes, plastics—and even perfume. We use fuel when we make a journey, a 'phone call, or take a bath. Our modern life makes great demands on our store of fuel. How much is there left? What will we do when the store runs out? In this book John Thomas tells us about the ways we find fuel and how we use it—and what we must do to save it.

What goes on in a power station, and how do geologists find coal, oil and gas under the ground—and the sea? What exactly is nuclear power, and how safe is it? This book gives you all the answers.

Science in Action

THE QUEST FOR FUEL

John A G Thomas

Wayland

Other books in this series

SBN 85340 619 7
Copyright © 1978 Wayland Publishers Limited
First published in 1978 by
Wayland Publishers Limited, 49 Lansdowne Place, Hove, East Sussex BN3 1HF
Phototypeset by Direct Image, Hove
Printed by Butler & Tanner Ltd, Frome and London

Frontispiece *Mechanical roof supports
help miners in this colliery in Warwickshire,
England.*

Contents

1 Fuel in your life

We are used to having plenty of fuel. Our lives are full of products from oil, gas and coal. We use fuel all the time. Look around you. How would things change if you were living in a world without oil, gas, coal and electricity?

It would be no use flicking a switch at night. Our light would have to be candle-light. Your meals would be cold unless they were cooked on an open fire of sticks gathered from the woods. Life would be quieter—no traffic noise, no road drills, no radio, hi-fi or TV. But it would be uncomfortable for us: we would freeze in the winter and swelter in the summer. We could travel only as far as we could walk. There would be no road vehicles, trains or aircraft—only our feet, and horses!

In your schoolroom, or home—how many light bulbs are there, how many heaters or air conditioners that you rely on? What special equipment is there which uses fuel,

Concorde *refuels at Dubai International Airport. Modern air travel demands vast amounts of fuel.*

like cookers, TV, projectors, swimming pools, electric bells? If we all had to cut our use of fuel, it would drastically change our lives.

We use fuel to make carpets, chairs, clothes, medicines and many, many more things—modern people would find life very hard without them. We have come to rely so much on fuel that we find it hard to imagine life with less.

The control room at London Weekend Television. TV is just one of our many modern luxuries which use fuel.

7

Above *Fuel before the Oil Age.* Long before man drilled for oil or dug for coal, he gathered wood for the fire.

Left *Fuel in the Oil Age.* These crew members aboard Sea Quest, *BP's* drilling platform in the North Sea, are operating clamps that hold the drill in place.

Above *A tailor's shop four hundred years ago. The tailor is cutting cloth to make another cloak like the one on the wall. The man at the back of the room is sewing seams by hand.*

Above right *Inside a modern factory making clothes. The machines, lighting, heating and air system depend on fuel.*

Below *A boot-and-shoe-maker four hundred years ago. He cuts and sews the leather by hand.*

Right *Making shoes the modern way. The machines use fuel, and so does the machine which made the machines . . . .*

2 We need fuel for . . .

heating and lighting

Since earliest times, people have warmed themselves in front of fires. Wood was the fuel first used, followed by coal. Most new homes these days have central heating, which uses a central burner run on oil, gas or solid fuel. The heat is passed round the house as warm water to radiators, or as warm air through ducts and vents. *Natural gas* is very good for heating homes, because it is easy and clean. Oil is used in large buildings and factories.

Fuel is needed for cooling as well. We use refrigerators to store vegetables, meat, milk and ice-cream. In hot climates we use massive amounts of fuel to keep homes, offices, cars and shops cool.

Right *A new type of coal fire. The fire burns smokeless fuel and heats enough water for eight radiators, baths and washing up.*

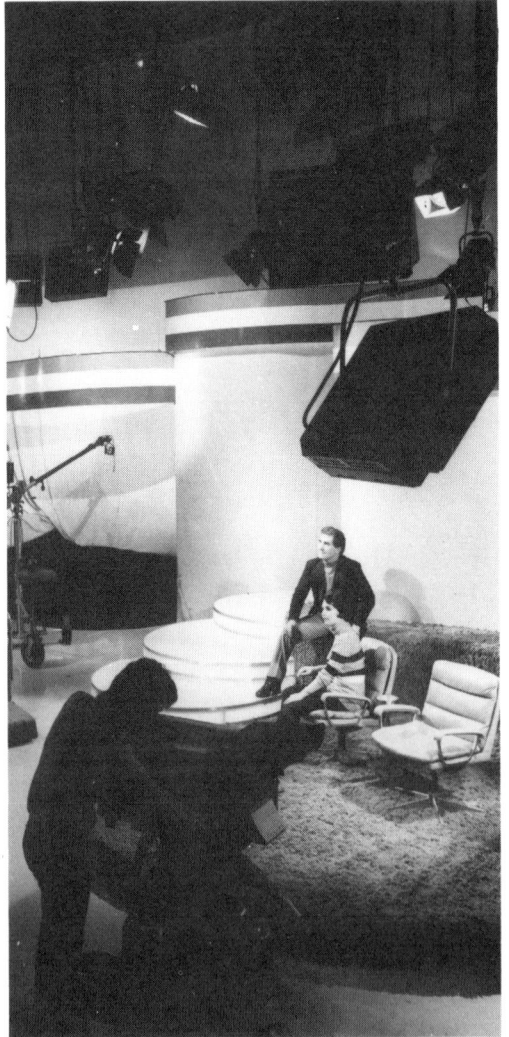

Right *We use lighting at home and at work, in travel and in leisure. Here the bright lights shine in a television studio.*

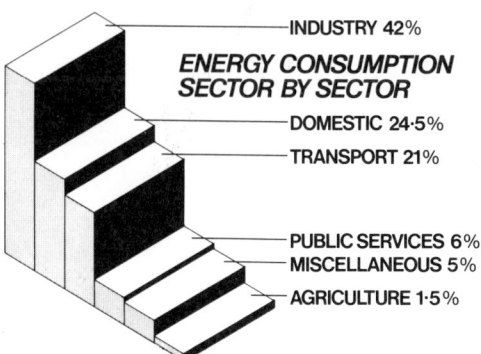

ENERGY CONSUMPTION
SECTOR BY SECTOR

- INDUSTRY 42%
- DOMESTIC 24·5%
- TRANSPORT 21%
- PUBLIC SERVICES 6%
- MISCELLANEOUS 5%
- AGRICULTURE 1·5%

Electric lighting is an essential part of life in all industrialized countries. Lighting has become more efficient over the years. The fluorescent tube converts 20% of the electricity it uses into light — the old glowing filament bulb uses only 5% and the rest is waste heat. We enjoy watching floodlit games. Lighting helps us travel, on the roads, at sea and in the air.

transport

In only one person's lifetime, oil has completely changed land, sea and air transport. The motor car sets the pace in many countries — particularly the USA. There, in the world's most mobile society, 25% of all energy goes in transport, 75% of this in road transport. Over 50% of all the transport energy in the USA is used by the motor car.

Many people object to the way in which the car dominates our cities and our lives. Cars need lots of space, for parks, garages and roads. More cars mean more exhaust pollution and scrap metal dumps. The cost of oil has made petrol (gasoline) very expensive. Scientists are looking for alternatives to the ordinary engine.

Left, above *and* below *Busy roads like these have changed the face of our cities and much of the countryside. Cars are a convenient form of transport, but make great demands for space and money — as well as fuel.*

Right *and* below *These vans are powered by electricity. In many countries there are vehicles run on gas. The scientists are trying to find a cheap, quick car that is quieter and cleaner than the kind run on petrol (gasoline).*

Electric delivery vehicles have been around for years. They run on electric batteries. The problem is that cars run on batteries can only travel quite short distances — about 80km (50 miles). Then they need recharging. In older models, acceleration is poor. There are many such vehicles on the market, and great improvements are being made all the time.

Normal car fuel will probably be scarce by the year 2000. Other types of engine, like steam- and gas-turbine engines, are being researched. New fuel alternatives are hydrogen and methyl alcohol. Changes in the car will come, but quite slowly because of all the investment in making, servicing and fuelling normal cars.

industry

Industry is the biggest user of fuel. All the developed countries use fuel to keep up their high standard of living. In the UK, for example, industry uses about 45% of all the energy produced.

Large amounts of fuel are needed in the steel industry. Here metal sheets are being made from ingots.

Left *Oil refining is another fuel-hungry industry. This phenol plant is at the Stanlow refinery, in Cheshire, England.*

Some industries use more energy than others. The main energy "guzzlers" in industry are these:

    iron and steel

    aluminium and other metals

    chemicals

    cement

    paper and packaging

These industries use processes that need a lot of heat. For example, the blast furnace, the hot-metal rolling mill and the oil refinery need lots of energy to produce heat.

This refinery is in the Netherlands. Like all industries, oil refining needs fuel for heating and lighting as well.

3 How long will it last?

Most energy experts agree about the broad trends. Some people forecast a great future for alternative energy sources. These sources include solar, geothermal, wind, tidal, and wave power. Many governments are looking into these. In the UK for example, an official survey predicts that in the year 2000, about

Right (above) *Drilling for oil off Venezuela. Oil will be running out by the year 2000.*

(Middle) *A solar panel being constructed. Solar energy will be more and more important.*

Right (below) *The prototype fast reactor at Dounteay, Caithness, Scotland. Fast breeder reactors could be producing power later in this century.*

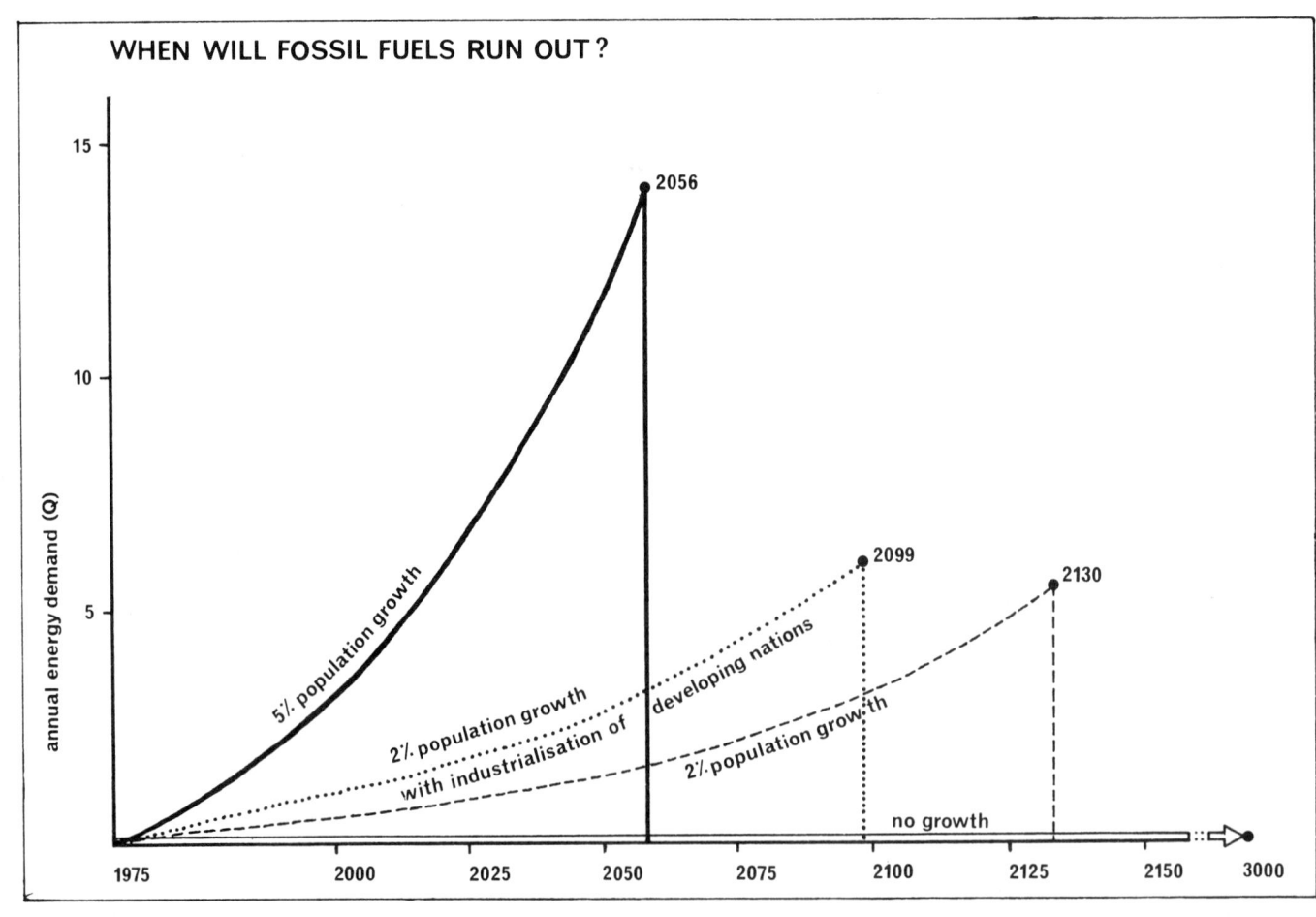

WHEN WILL FOSSIL FUELS RUN OUT?

annual energy demand (Q)

5% population growth — 2056

2% population growth with industrialisation of developing nations — 2099

2% population growth — 2130

no growth

1975 2000 2025 2050 2075 2100 2125 2150 3000

7% of all the energy needed will come from alternative sources. Over half of this will come from tides and waves.

the next ten years

Oil, natural gas and coal will continue to be our main energy sources. Nuclear fission will provide an increasing amount of our electricity. We shall have to *conserve* energy by using it wisely.

ten to twenty years

Oil and natural gas will start to run short. Coal will be made into oil and gas. Oil will be taken from *oil shales* and *tar sands.* Nuclear fission will provide a large part of our electricity. *Solar heating* and cooling will be common in buildings. Wave power may generate small amounts of electricity in countries with suitable coastlines.

the year 2000 and beyond

Nuclear fusion may be important. So might *geothermal power.* The *fast breeder reactor* (FBR) will probably have taken over from the older types of fission reactors. Solar power stations for generating electricity will be popular.

17

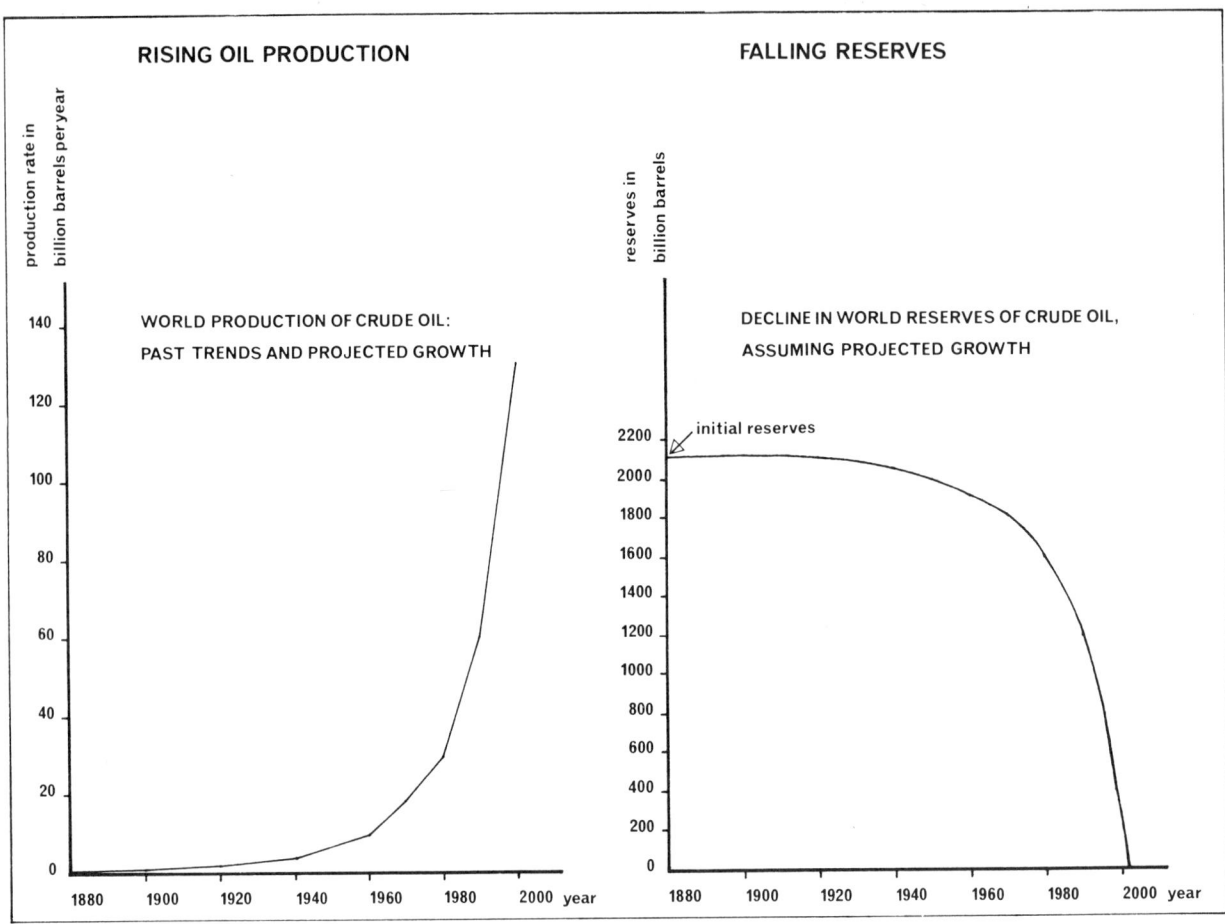

RISING OIL PRODUCTION

FALLING RESERVES

production rate in billion barrels per year

WORLD PRODUCTION OF CRUDE OIL:
PAST TRENDS AND PROJECTED GROWTH

reserves in billion barrels

DECLINE IN WORLD RESERVES OF CRUDE OIL,
ASSUMING PROJECTED GROWTH

initial reserves

We cannot be sure when the oil or gas will run out, but it will not happen suddenly. Even if no new reserves are found, much more oil could be taken from the wells we have. Oil engineers are working on methods to increase the amount taken. The method, and the research, is very expensive.

As supplies become scarce we will look harder for new sources. We can be fairly certain that oil and gas will last twenty years. Scientists will know more about the newer energy sources by that time.

waste not, want not

If we make a great effort to use energy more efficiently, all our supplies will last a lot longer. When energy was cheap (its price actually fell in the 1950s and 1960s) we saw no need for economy. Oil prices have increased by six times since then. The industrialized countries waste 15-20% of their energy. Houses can save energy by better insulation; industry can save by using more efficient machinery, and by using equipment with more sensitive controls.

Even if everyone works hard to save energy, results will be slow in coming. New houses are insulated when they are built— old ones were not. Industry has inefficient machines which it cannot afford to scrap. The earth's energy resources are finite. It is wrong for the industrial countries to waste these. The larger part of the world's population live in poor countries which use very little fuel at present. But they will need fuel in the future.

This man is laying a mineral fibre insulation roll in his loft. It is important to stop precious heat from escaping through the roof.

4 Can we find new sources, and in time?

All our energy comes from the sun. Green plants use the sun's energy to make food, in a process called *photosynthesis.* When we eat we draw on the sun's energy. If we eat plant food we use energy more directly than if we eat meat. Animals convert plants into flesh. When we eat meat we waste up to 90% of the energy.

Coal, gas and oil were formed millions of years ago by rotting plant and animal matter. When we burn them we release stored energy from the sun. As these *fossil fuels* run out, we must find new sources to replace them. Some alternatives to fossil fuels are less wasteful because we use the sun's energy directly. This is called solar energy. Solar panels, water-heaters and furnaces are already being used.

The immense heat of the earth's crust can be used as a source of energy. So can the movement of waves, tides and winds.

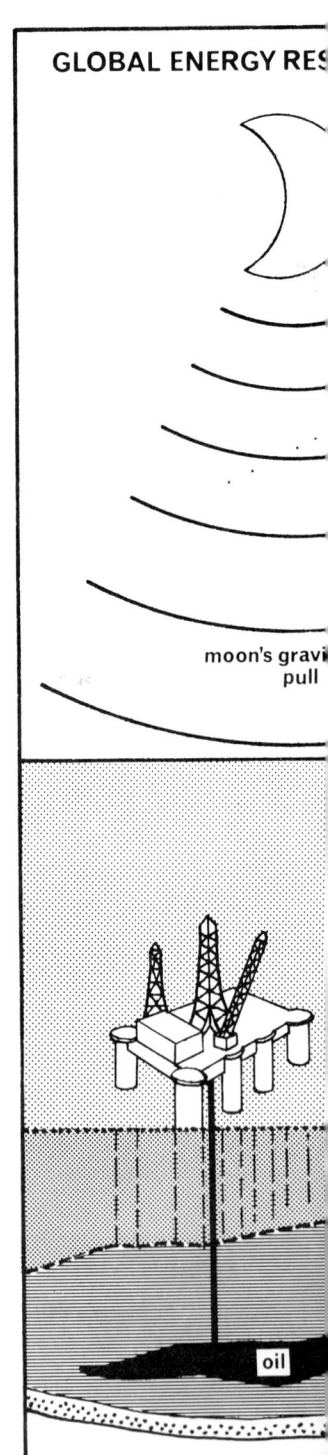

GLOBAL ENERGY RES

moon's gravi
pull

oil

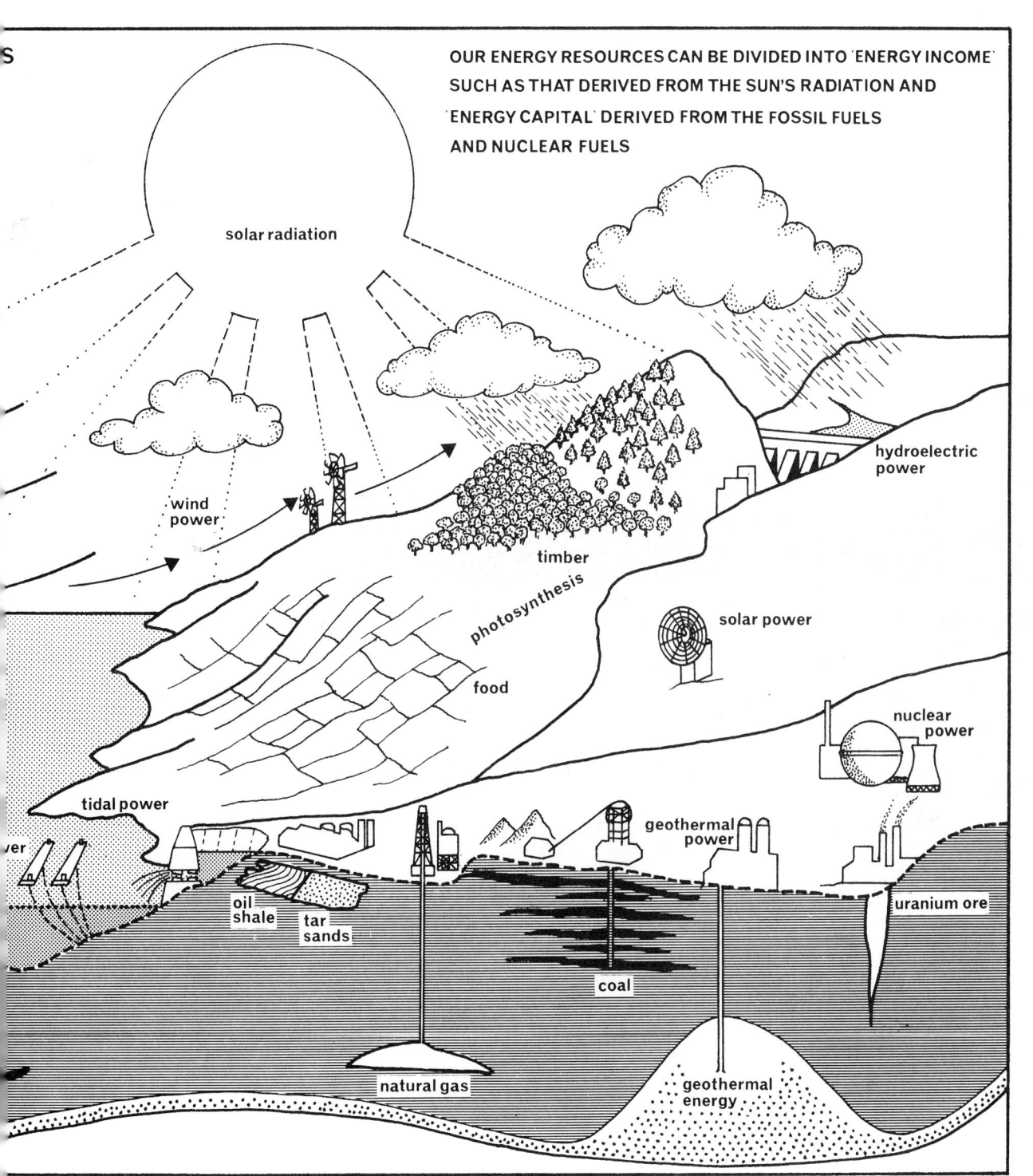

OUR ENERGY RESOURCES CAN BE DIVIDED INTO 'ENERGY INCOME' SUCH AS THAT DERIVED FROM THE SUN'S RADIATION AND 'ENERGY CAPITAL' DERIVED FROM THE FOSSIL FUELS AND NUCLEAR FUELS

solar radiation

wind power

timber

photosynthesis

food

solar power

hydroelectric power

nuclear power

tidal power

geothermal power

uranium ore

oil shale

tar sands

coal

natural gas

geothermal energy

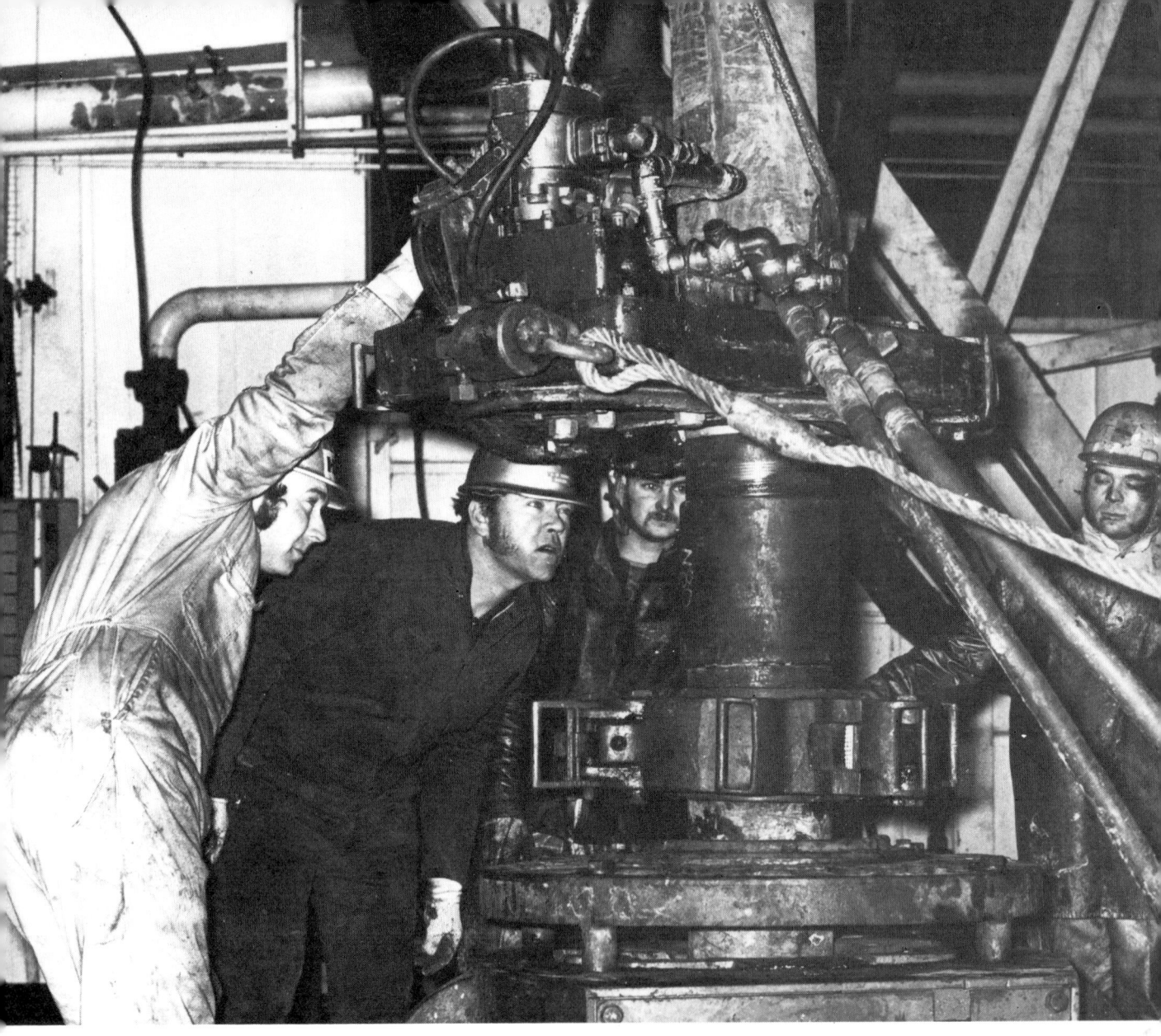

Many governments and international organizations are looking into these alternatives. This research is very costly, but we must quickly find replacements for fossil fuels.

There is large investment in the Oil industry. These men are working aboard the Ocean Voyager *offshore from the UK. Despite better exploring and production methods, eventually the oil will run out.*

5 Coal—dirty but plentiful

The United Kingdom, the pioneer industrial nation, grew up with coal in the period 1750-1850. Coal raised the steam in the boilers of the early steam engines. Today, 60% of the UK's electricity is generated with coal. The open coal fire has almost disappeared, and is being replaced by central heating.

This early steam engine, called a whimsey, was used to haul coal in a Staffordshire colliery.

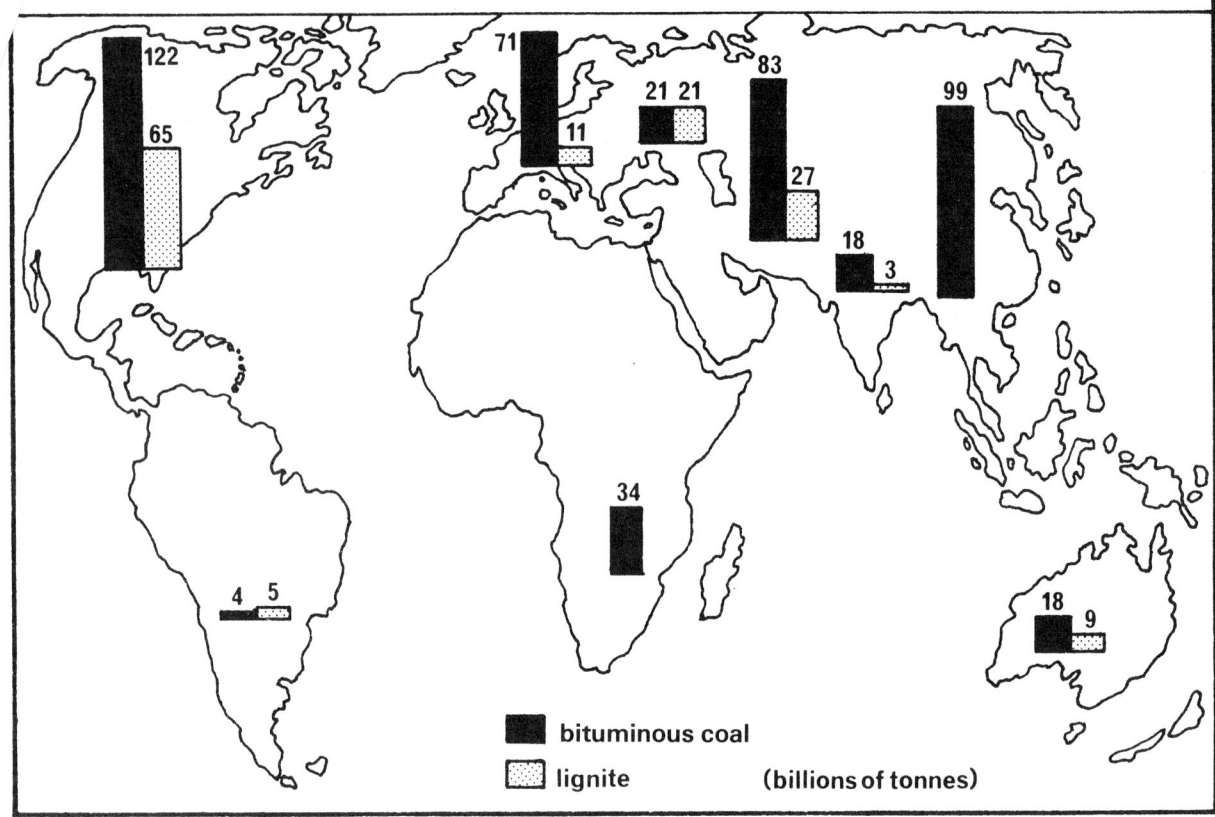

ECONOMICALLY RECOVERABLE COAL RESERVES

122

65

71

11

21 21

83

27

99

18
3

18
9

34

4 5

■ bituminous coal

▨ lignite   (billions of tonnes)

Coal is by far the most abundant fossil fuel. But it is expensive and dirty to mine. Since the end of 1973 when oil prices rose suddenly, coal has made a comeback for two reasons. Coal reserves are spread out all over the world. Politics need not come in to it—everyone can use their own. With oil, however, the Arab states which own the largest reserves can control supply to other countries. There is also the price of oil to be considered; coal is a better bargain with oil prices rising.

This diagram shows the amount of coal (in billions of tonnes) which can be recovered by the methods we now use. Bituminous coal is black household coal. Lignite is brown and crumbly.

open-cast or strip-mining

This method of mining is easier and cheaper than deep mining. It is only possible to open-cast mine (or strip-mine as the Americans say) where the coal lies near the surface. It also needs to be in thick seams. A giant scoop removes the earth over the seam and then gouges out the coal. It is a quick method, and needs fewer skilled workers than deep mining.

Below *An opencast coal mining site near Walsall, England. This method of mining is less dangerous than deep mining, because the miners don't need to go underground. But it makes a mess of the land and spoils the beauty of the countryside.*

The USA, USSR, Australia, Germany and Poland use this method on a large scale. Often special permission is needed before open-cast mining can begin. It is likely to cover a large area and will look ugly. Most landowners insist that the land is restored when mining is finished. This means re-grassing, planting trees and re-building roads. This is expensive, but then open-cast mining is cheap, safe and quick.

Transport underground is automatic. The locomotive is linked by radio to the control room at the pithead.

These powered supports hold up the coal roof while the shearer takes off a strip of coal.

Conveyor belts move coal to the bunkers in the modern mine. The coal has already been screened into large and small sizes.

deep mining

Often the coal is deep under the ground and mine-shafts have to be dug. In the *deep mine* there are mechanical pit props which hold the roof up, and move along as the coal is cut. The mechanical cutters remove the coal in long strips. They are operated by miners, but take much of the hard work out of winning the coal. The days of the pick and shovel are gone!

The cut coal falls onto a conveyor belt which takes it to the shaft. From here it goes in 20-ton skips to the surface. In the USA, shuttle cars carry the coal instead of conveyor belts and skips. All this mechanization cuts the numbers of miners needed, but mining is still a dangerous job.

oil and gas from coal

Oil and natural gas are easy to use and transport. Oil is essential as a fuel for aircraft and most ships. At present it is needed to run cars. There is at least ten times more coal than either oil or gas in the world. It therefore makes sense to look for ways of making oil and gas from coal.

Small plants for making gas from coal have been built. They will be in full production by 1980, especially in the USA. Many oil-from-coal plants were built in Germany during World War II. South Africa has no oilfields and has made oil from coal since 1955. The question is, what methods would be used? And will the cost be low enough?

made from coal. In the future we are likely to see "coal refineries" or "coalplexes" with power stations attached. The coalplex will provide gas, oil, and chemicals, and also electricity.

This conveyor belt is taking mixed-size coal direct from the coal face to be screened.

The powerful shearer at work on the face. It's much quicker than a pick and shovel—and easier, too!

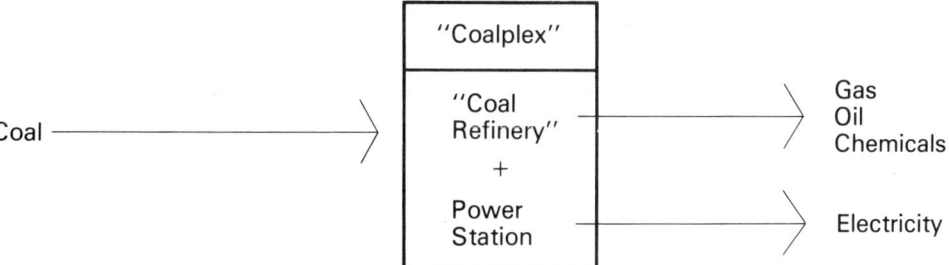

Coal ⟶ "Coalplex" — "Coal Refinery" + Power Station ⟶ Gas, Oil, Chemicals ⟶ Electricity

problems with coal

When coal is burned, particles of carbon, (soot) are given off in the smoke. Compounds of carbon and hydrogen are also given off. These can be removed. It is much harder to remove sulphur dioxide, the invisible corrosive gas that is often there.

Above *Manchester, England in Victorian times. The factories burned coal for fuel and "... the air and soil are full of fog and soot. Factories with blackened bricks stand in rows like prisons".*

Right *These briquettes are a kind of smokeless fuel called "Homefire".*

Many smokeless fuels are now made from coal. When these burn there is no smoke and little dust or ash. But sulphur dioxide still goes up the chimney.

6 Oil and gas

the search

Oil and natural gas have been formed over millions of years in the earth's crust. Marine organisms trapped in certain rock formations in *sedimentary basins* have slowly been converted into oil and gas. Occasionally the rocks have prevented the escape of the oil and gas and an oil field was formed. The geologist looking for oil can find out if oil is likely to be found but drilling is the only true test. Gas is always found with oil and sometimes alone.

Right *The oil rig* Ocean Voyager *in the storm-tossed North Sea. You can see the platform for helicopters to land, and the tall drilling derrick which controls the drill itself. Men eat well and have cosy cabins aboard, but the work is very hard and dangerous. Ships and helicopters serve the rigs with supplies, and also keep watch in case a man falls overboard. In these cold and rough seas, a man could only stay alive for a few minutes.*

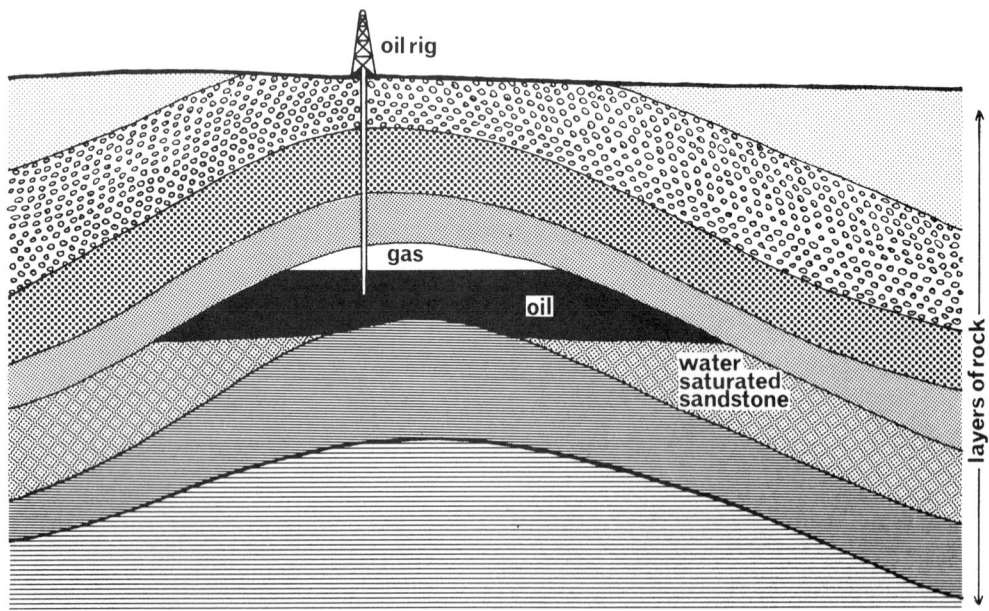

oil rig

gas

oil

water saturated sandstone

layers of rock

ANTICLINE TRAP
SHOWING GAS, OIL AND WATER LAYERS

The oil under the North Sea has brought new wealth to the countries which found it. British Petroleum (BP) say that 20,000-25,000 million barrels of oil lie in the UK sector alone. But the reserves in the North Sea are only a small fraction of the world's total oil store. Nearly 60% of our reserves lie in the Middle East.

Below *A diagram showing the main parts of an oil and gas drilling rig. The flare stack is for burning off gas.*

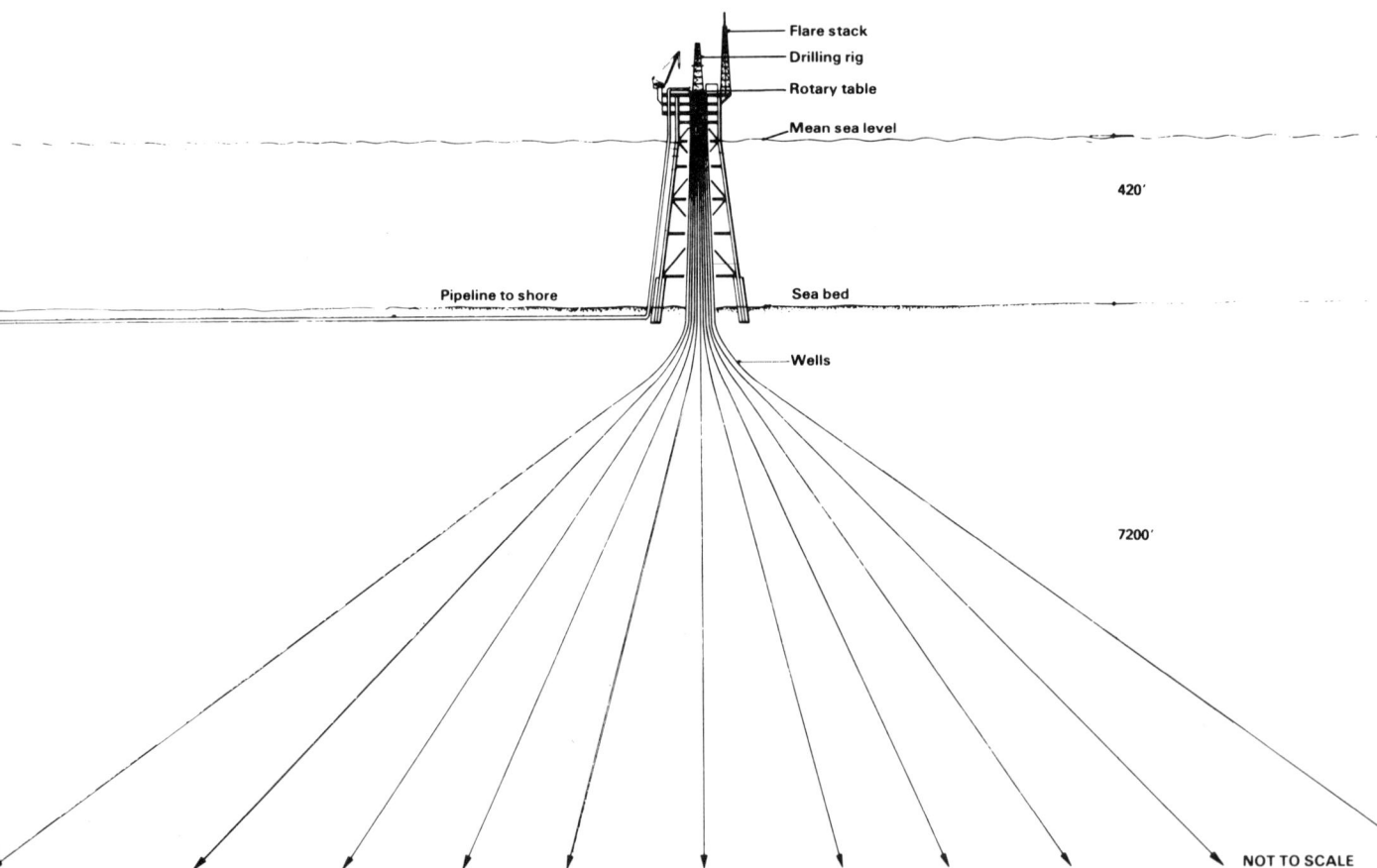

Flare stack
Drilling rig
Rotary table
Mean sea level
420'
Pipeline to shore
Sea bed
Wells
7200'
NOT TO SCALE

Above *The* SS Megare, *an oil tanker built in Japan. Oil is easier to transport in tankers than gas, because gas has to be liquidized under pressure. A shipwrecked oil tanker causes pollution, but a gas tanker collision would cause a gigantic explosion.*

oil

Oil is easy to transport. Because it is liquid, it can be pumped through pipes, and carried by tankers. This makes it more attractive than coal. Oil often has to be brought long distances from the deserts of the Middle East. It goes overland by pipeline and then in large tankers to the refineries.

Road tankers load at the refinery depot. They carry fuel oil and gas oil produced at the refinery.

Above right A tank farm at Zarzaitine, Algeria, by night. Here the crude oil is stored before being piped to the refinery.

In the *refinery,* crude oil (the oil from the well) is boiled and condensed at different temperatures. This gives a range of oil products, ranging from car and aircraft fuel to diesel and heating oil. These oil products are taken by road tanker to the consumer. Oil is also the source of chemicals used to make paints, plastics and dyes.

Right Simple distillation of crude oil in the refinery gives rise to wide range of products. Low-boiling-point products emerge from the top of the distillation column.

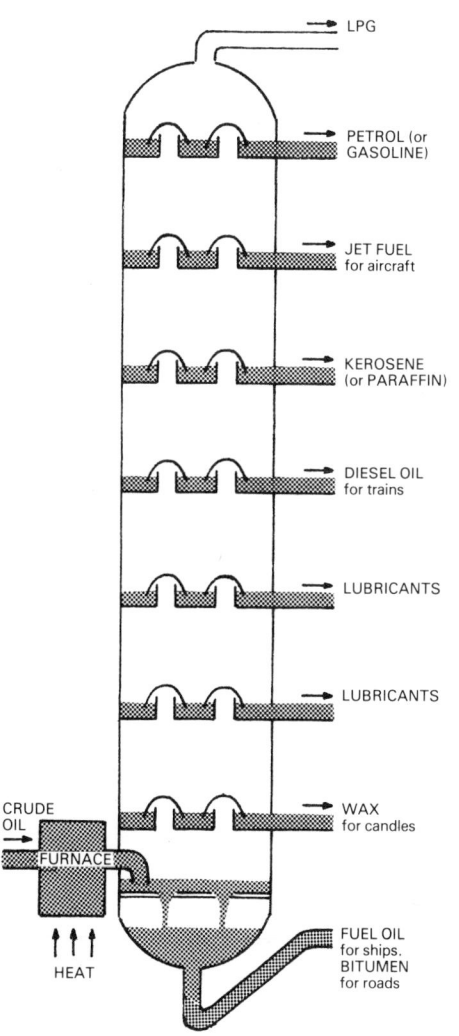

LPG

PETROL (or
GASOLINE)

JET FUEL
for aircraft

KEROSENE
(or PARAFFIN)

DIESEL OIL
for trains

LUBRICANTS

LUBRICANTS

WAX
for candles

CRUDE
OIL

FURNACE

HEAT

FUEL OIL
for ships.
BITUMEN
for roads

Oil geologists do not expect to find such a rich field as that in the Middle East. The only possible area where very large deposits of oil could still be found is in northern Siberia, USSR.

The oil will not run out suddenly. More oil can be taken from existing wells using more expensive methods. The oil is forced to the surface by the pressure of gas in the reservoir. That leaves 80% of the oil in the ground. By pumping air, gas or water in the well, 10% more can be taken. Total USA reserves are 430,000 million barrels. By ordinary methods, only 140,000 millions will be taken—leaving 67% in the wells! There are new methods being tested which can take more oil. New deposits will be more difficult to find. Oil will be more expensive. It looks as though we will begin to run short by the year 2000.

natural gas

Natural gas was found in vast quantities at Groningen near the Dutch coast in 1959. This find led to the discovery of North Sea oil.

Natural gas is an ideal fuel. It is clean to burn and wastes little energy. It is not poisonous like the old coal gas (which was made from coal). Natural gas from the North Sea now supplies the Netherlands, Belgium, France, Germany and the UK. Its use in the UK has doubled since 1959. It provides nearly 16% of the total energy used there.

Unfortunately supplies are limited. Europe will have to look for other sources to meet growing demands. One answer would be to transport it in special ships from the Middle East. It would come from Syria, Libya, and Algeria in liquid form. This is liquefied natural gas, or LNG.

A pipeline can only carry 20% as much gas as oil, when we consider its heating value. One "pipeline-full" of oil would boil five times as many kettles of water as one "pipeline-full" of natural gas. Shipping LNG

*Gas produced in Brunei, Borneo, is liquefied
and then loaded onto special ships. Here the
SS Gardinia loads with LNG (liquefied
natural gas) to take to Japan.*

costs about nine times as much as shipping crude oil. These costs make importing gas look less attractive.

This tanker is being built with five spherical tanks to hold LNG. The gas will be kept at minus 290°F, and go from Algeria to the USA.

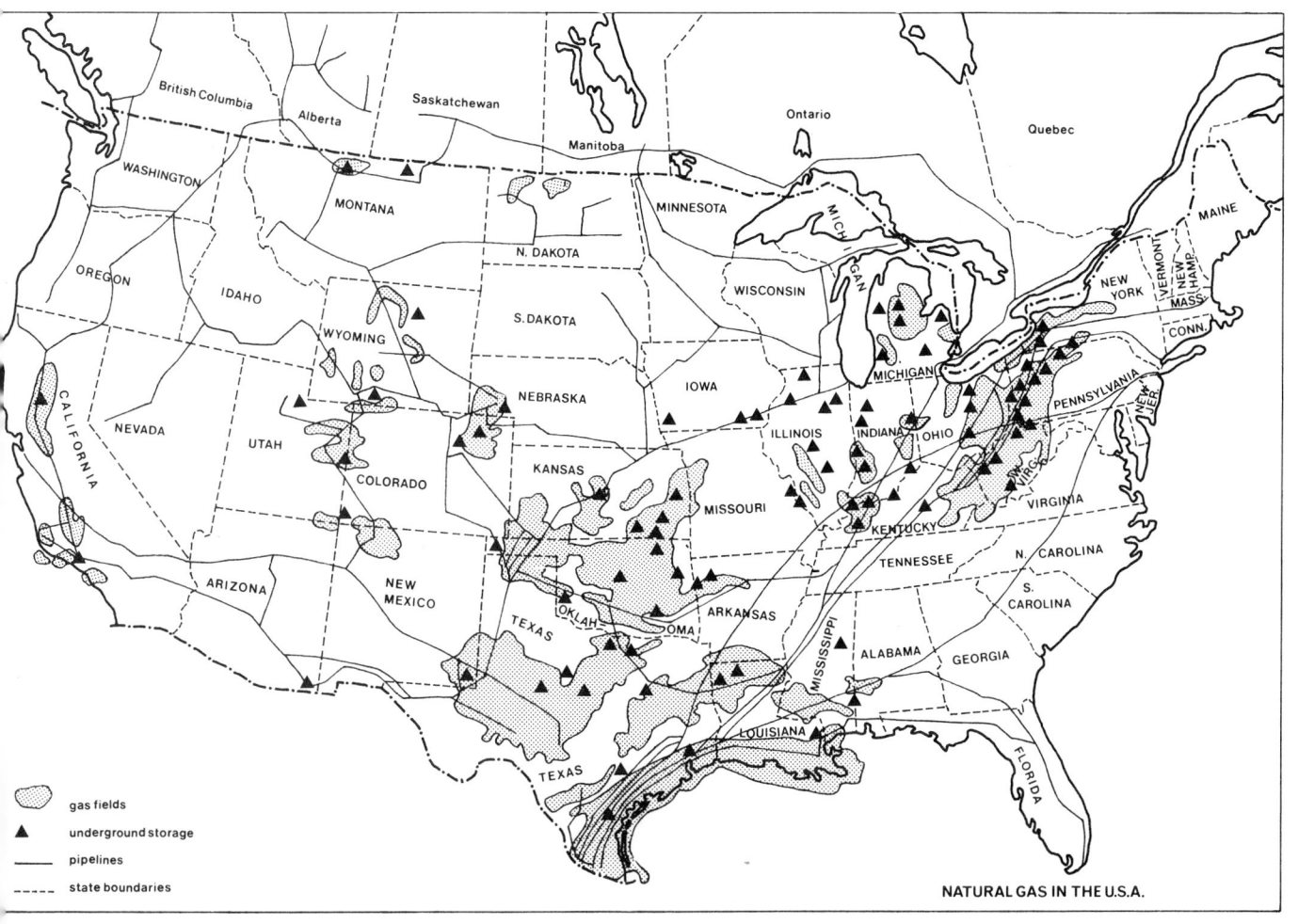

gas fields
▲ underground storage
—— pipelines
----- state boundaries

NATURAL GAS IN THE U.S.A.

Natural gas is very important in the USA. It supplies about 30% of all USA energy needs. Over 40% of all homes are heated by natural gas. Supplies are already dwindling, however, and in some parts of the USA gas is rationed. In the future, gas will have to be made from coal.

7 Electricity

electricity from fossil fuels

Unlike coal, oil, gas (and uranium, as we shall see), electricity is a secondary form of energy. It is manufactured from these other fuels. It is usually made by boiling water to produce steam which turns steam turbines

Above The turbine hall in the coal-fired power station at Eggborough, Yorkshire, England.

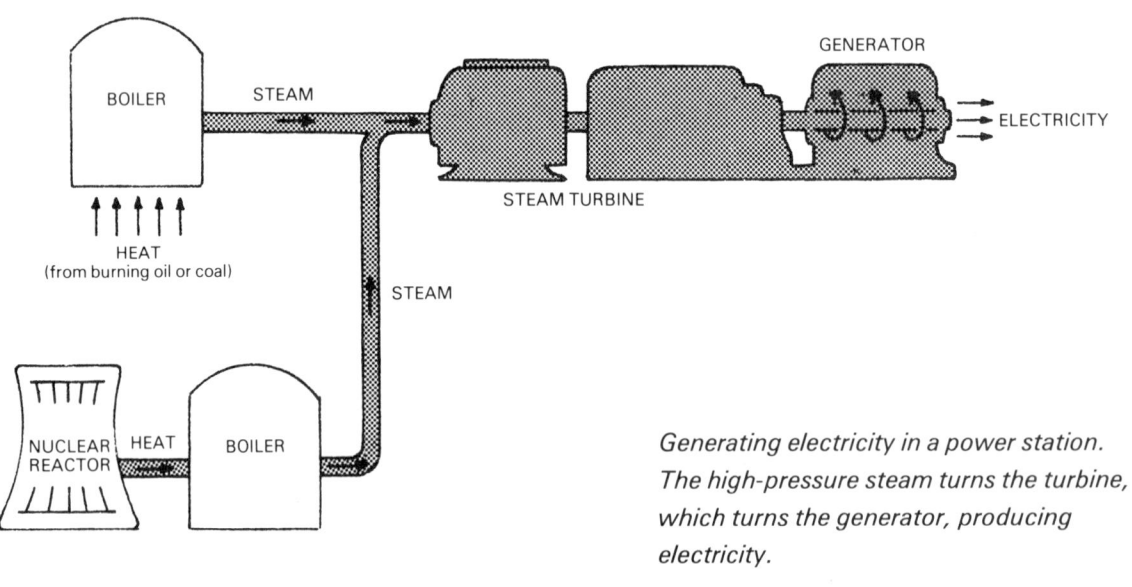

Generating electricity in a power station. The high-pressure steam turns the turbine, which turns the generator, producing electricity.

in a power station. There are three main parts to a power station:

1 A furnace burning coal, oil, or (much less often) natural gas. Or a nuclear reactor with uranium as the fuel. The heat is used to boil water, which makes steam.

2 A steam turbine, which is a motor turned by a jet of high-pressure steam, in much the same way as water turns a water-wheel.

3 An electric generator connected to the turbine which it turns. The generator consists of coils of copper wire between the poles of a powerful magnet. When the coils are turned an electric current flows.

Below *The main station of the coal-fired power station at Drax, Yorkshire, England. There are six 114m cooling towers. Water comes from the River Ouse.*

Above *Here a 400kV cable is being taken across the River Wye in England. Laying cables out of sight looks better, but is far more expensive.*

Left *Pylons carrying 400 kV from Sizewell power station. You can see that crops can be grown under and around the pylons.*

When the electricity has been generated, it is conducted through cables. These run above the ground strung between pylons or underground in pipes. Pylons look ugly but it costs about sixteen times more to lay cables out of sight. In most countries a national grid system links all the electricity generating stations.

electricity from water

Electricity can also be generated by driving water turbines with falling water. They are the modern water-wheels. The turbines then drive generators. The system produces

Above *The Ffestiniog pumped storage scheme in Merionethshire, Wales, consists of two reservoirs at different levels. The upper reservoir is an enlargment of the natural mountain lake Llyn Stwlan. The lower reservoir was formed by damming the River Afon Ystradau. The power station is built of local stone, and was opened by Queen Elizabeth II in 1963.*

Above *The Rheidol hydro-electric scheme
station in Wales. The station produces
56 MW. The power for the scheme comes in
the rainwater that falls on the surrounding
rugged mountainside.*

hydro-electricity. It does not cause pollution
—no fuel is burned—and the water it uses is
free. Most of the suitable sites for hydro-
electric schemes have been used up in the
developed countries. There are many sites
waiting for development in Africa, South
America and southern Asia.

One great problem with electricity is that it cannot be stored. It must be generated twenty-four hours a day. When demand is low, electric pumps move water from a lower reservoir to a higher one. When

Right *The turbine hall at Ffestiniog power station.*

Below *One of the four generator/motors in the turbine pit. These machines are rated at 90 MW.*

demand is heavy—such as when most people are cooking dinner—the water in the upper reservoir is allowed to rush down. It turns a water turbine and generates electricity. This "instant" power source is called *pumped water storage.*

Below *The No 1 storage pump at Ffestiniog.*

electricity from nuclear fission

Coal, oil and gas give off heat when burned. The chemical energy in the fuels is converted into heat energy. In a *nuclear reactor,* the nucleus of the atom is split, in a process called *fission.* For the same weight of fuel, nuclear energy releases more than a million times more heat than chemical energy. This can be released destructively in atom bombs, or to generate heat in a power station.

The nucleus of an atom is made up of protons (positively charged particles) and neutrons (uncharged particles). Uranium, a heavy metal, has 143 neutrons in its nucleus. When the nucleus is hit by a neutron, it splits and releases three neutrons, and a lot of heat. In a nuclear reactor, the neutrons are slowed down, so that the newly-released ones hit and split other nuclei. This is called a *controlled chain reaction.* It makes the nuclear reactor different from an atom bomb which owes its power to an *uncontrolled chain reaction.*

A diagram showing what happens at the start of a controlled chain reaction.

NEUTRON

URANIUM NUCLEUS

FISSION PRODUCTS

NEUTRONS

Calder Hall, one of the earliest nuclear power stations to be built in the UK.

The turbine hall in the prototype fast reactor at Caithness in Scotland.

Most of a nuclear power station is exactly the same as any other power station. The only difference is that the heat comes from a nuclear reactor rather than from a furnace burning coal, oil or gas. At the heart of the nuclear reactor are the uranium fuel rods. These are surrounded by graphite or "heavy water". There are also rods of boron. They can be put into the reactor or taken out to control the rate of reaction: boron absorbs neutrons.

The Steam Generating Heavy Water Reactor at Winfrith, Dorset, England. This power station produces 100 MW of electricity.

Above *The Advanced Gas-cooled Reactor at Windscale, England. This reactor uses Uranium oxide as fuel, and the gas leaves the cooling system 200°C higher than at Calder Hall— and so produces more electricity.*

Left *The Steam Generating Heavy Water Reactor at Winfrith. Here one of the fuel elements is being moved to storage.*

The middle of the reactor gets hot as soon as the chain reaction is under way. It is cooled by circulating as gas, carbon dioxide, or a liquid, normal or heavy water, which itself becomes hot. This heat is then used to boil water. The steam turns turbine-generators.

The nuclear industry is developing a new type of reactor called the Fast Breeder Reactor (FBR). It is more efficient. The FBR is so called because the neutrons are not slowed down. The nuclear fission generates (breeds) more fuel than is used up in the production of heat. The fuel is plutonium, an element made from uranium in the normal reactor. Uranium has to be mined and made into fuel rods. After a time in the

Below The diagram shows the working of the first nuclear power station built in the UK, at Calder Hall. The chain reaction has to happen at a steady rate. So, the number of neutrons which carry on the reaction have to be controlled. Boron absorbs excess neutrons, so boron Control Rods are used. The neutrons are slowed down by surrounding the uranium Fuel Element by a Moderator, in this case using graphite. The Concrete Shield prevents radiation escaping. The hot gas goes to make steam which drives electricity generators.

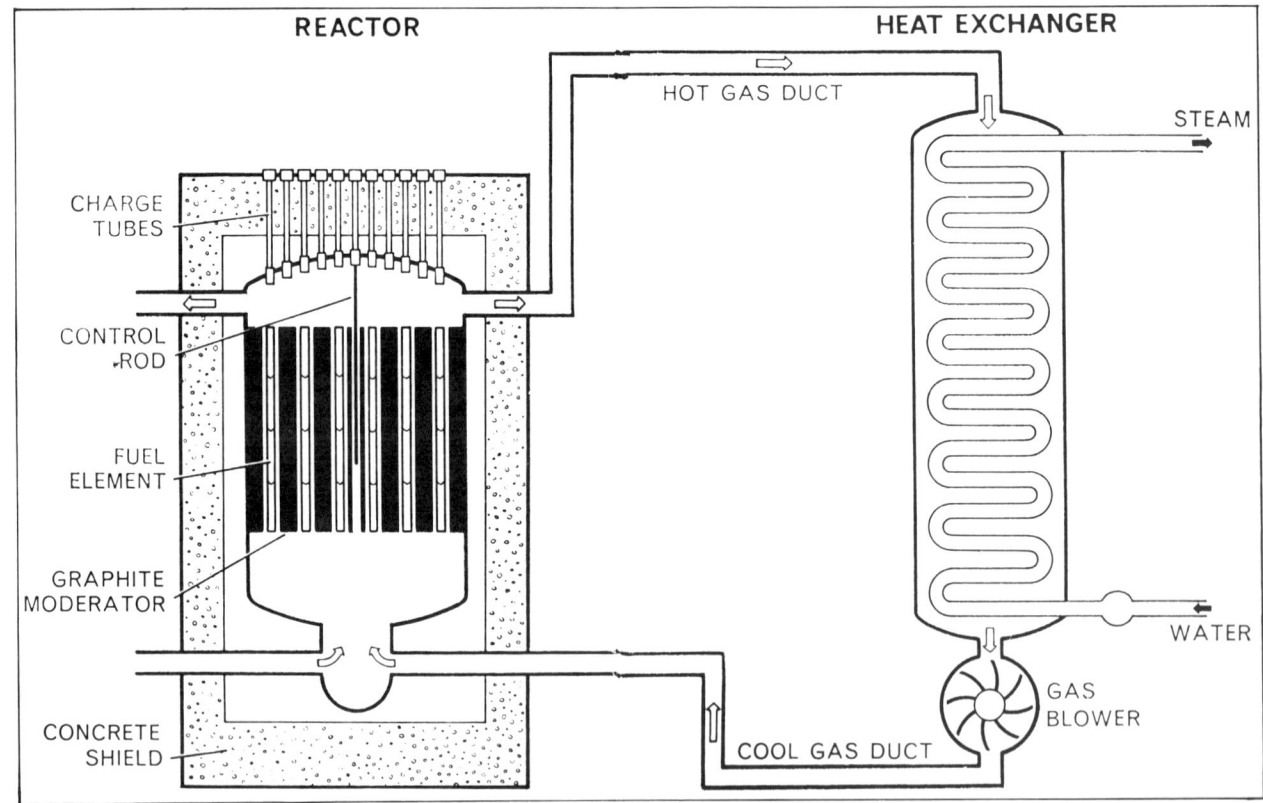

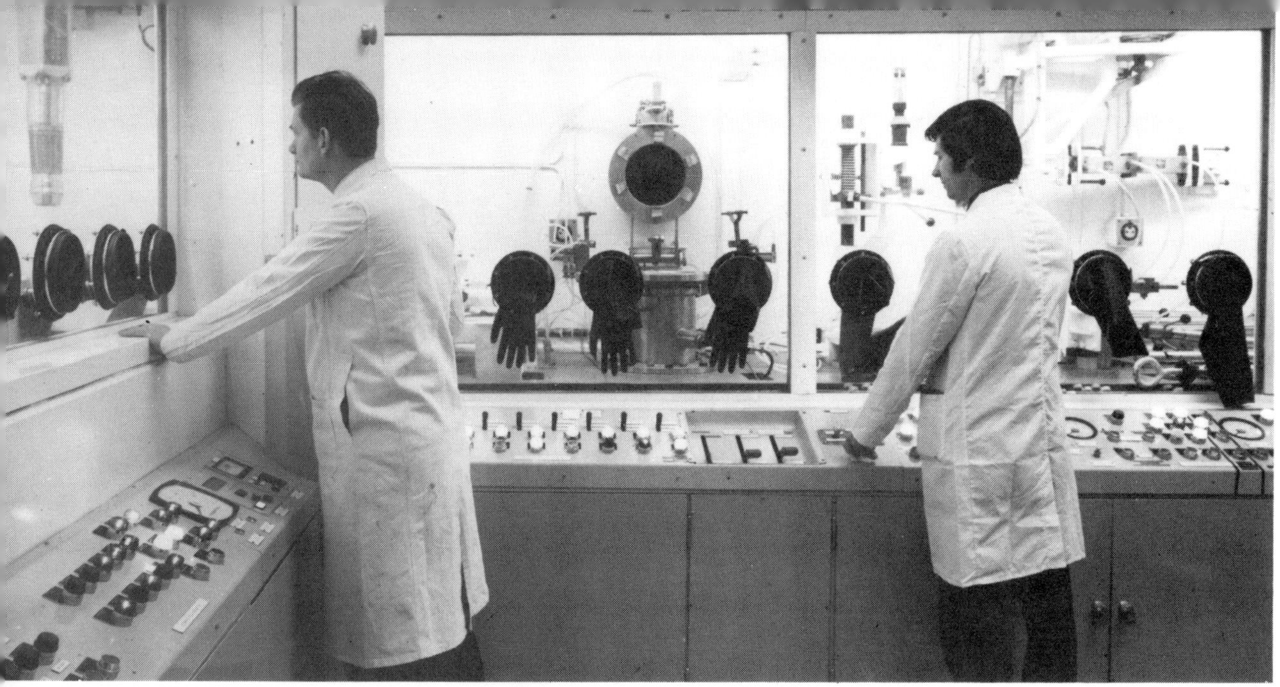

Above *Fuel is inspected before insertion into the Fast Reactor. The fuel is manufactured at Windscale and inspected by remote control at the Prototype Fast Reactor at Caithness, Scotland.*

The spent fuel from nuclear reactors is reprocessed at Windscale. The highly radioactive waste products are stored in steel tanks. This is one of the tanks.

reactor, the fuel is used up. It is removed and sent for reprocessing. Uranium, plutonium and the many products that are formed in the reactor are radioactive. This radiation cannot be seen, smelt or felt but it is very harmful. It causes cancer. Great care has to be taken all along the line—in handling, transportation and reprocessing.

The nuclear industry is very safety-minded. Some scientists feel that the risks are still too great, especially with the FBR. Some radioactive material remains dangerous for many thousands of years. One risk, however small, is that terrorists might steal plutonium and make a bomb.

The growth of nuclear power to make electricity depends on scientists and engineers—can they solve the remaining problems? It will also depend on public opinion. Are we prepared to accept the risks?

Above *Fast Reactor operators at the control desk at Caithness, Scotland. All the information needed to operate the station can be displayed on the five screens.*

Right *The Steam Generating Heavy Water Reactor at Winfrith has to be shut down for refuelling. The pressure tubes are being checked here.*

8 New Sources of power

The experts tell us that within the next twenty-five years we could be running short of fossil fuels. We are using up our store faster than we can find new reserves. We have to change the way we produce and use energy. We can start by being more careful with what we have. Sooner or later we must find new sources of power, heat and light. We can use the sun, the movement of water and wind, and the heat of the *earth's crust.* We can also use different energy sources like uranium for nuclear power, oil shale and tar sands.

Many countries are interested in solar energy. The UK has been researching into its use for years. This solar hot plate water heater is being tested on a roof in London.

solar energy

Using the sun's energy is very attractive. It produces little or no pollution, and the power source is free. The earth receives 167,000 times more energy from the sun than we now use from all other sources. Many countries, particularly Japan and the USA, are looking at ways of using the sun's energy.

Houses have already been built with solar panels on the roof. They absorb heat from the sun. The problem is that the sunshine comes and goes in many countries, and the heat is difficult to store. At present, fitting a house with solar panels to the roof is quite expensive. However, the price will fall when it becomes popular. The system soon pays for itself. The sun's energy can also be used to drive a cooling system. This makes a lot of sense since we need cooling when the sun is at its hottest. In the future we can expect to make good use of solar energy, especially at home.

We could use the sun's energy to make electricity in a power station. Lenses or mirrors larger than any we know would have to be built to concentrate the sun's rays.

Solar cells generate electricity when the sun shines on them. They were first made for spacecraft. At present they are much too expensive to use on earth. There are some special uses, though. The Solar Power Corporation in the USA sell them for use on boats. When the sun shines on them they generate electricity and charge a battery. When there is no sun, the battery

Solar collecting tubes like these provide energy from a free power source — the sun. They can go on the roofs of houses and give plenty of hot water.

can be used to provide power on the boat.

The sun's energy is now being taken seriously. It will probably be the next century before it is a large part of our total energy supply.

nuclear fusion

Nuclear fusion (not to be confused with nuclear fission) is the sun's own energy source. It is also the explosive force of the hydrogen bomb.

Fission is the spliting of the nucleus of a

Research goes on at the Culham Laboratory in England in fusion. The big injector shoots a beam of hydrogen atoms into the magnetic trap (opposite) to heat the plasma.

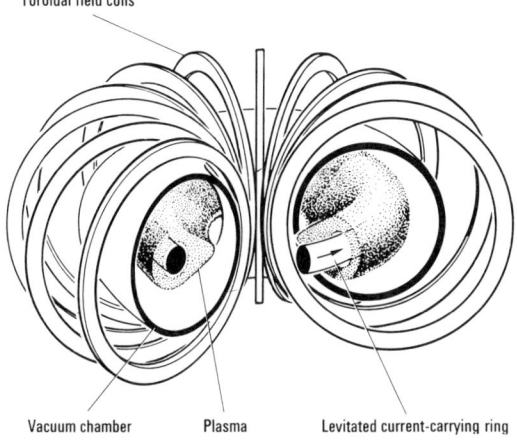

Diagram showing the kind of magnetic bottle, or trap, in which very hot hydrogen can be reacted.

Toroidal field coils

Vacuum chamber Plasma Levitated current-carrying ring

heavy atom. Fusion is the joining of the nuclei of two light atoms, usually hydrogen, deuterium or tritium. An enormous amount of energy, usually heat energy, is released when fusion takes place.

There are great problems in trying to copy the reactions that take place on the sun. It needs a temperature of 100 million degrees Centigrade. All materials melt at temperatures like this! Researchers are trying to make a "magnetic bottle" in which the very hot hydrogen can be reacted. No-one has yet proved that it can be done. The USA spent about £20 million in 1973 on the project. They plan to spend another £500 million up to 1980, and a further £2,500 million after that.

Another fusion machine uses laser power, a highly concentrated beam of light. This is also being studied.

The great advantage of fusion—if it can be made to work—is that we can get the fuel from sea water. Also there would be much less danger from radiation. If the scientists make their machines work, we may see fusion power generating electricity before the year 2000.

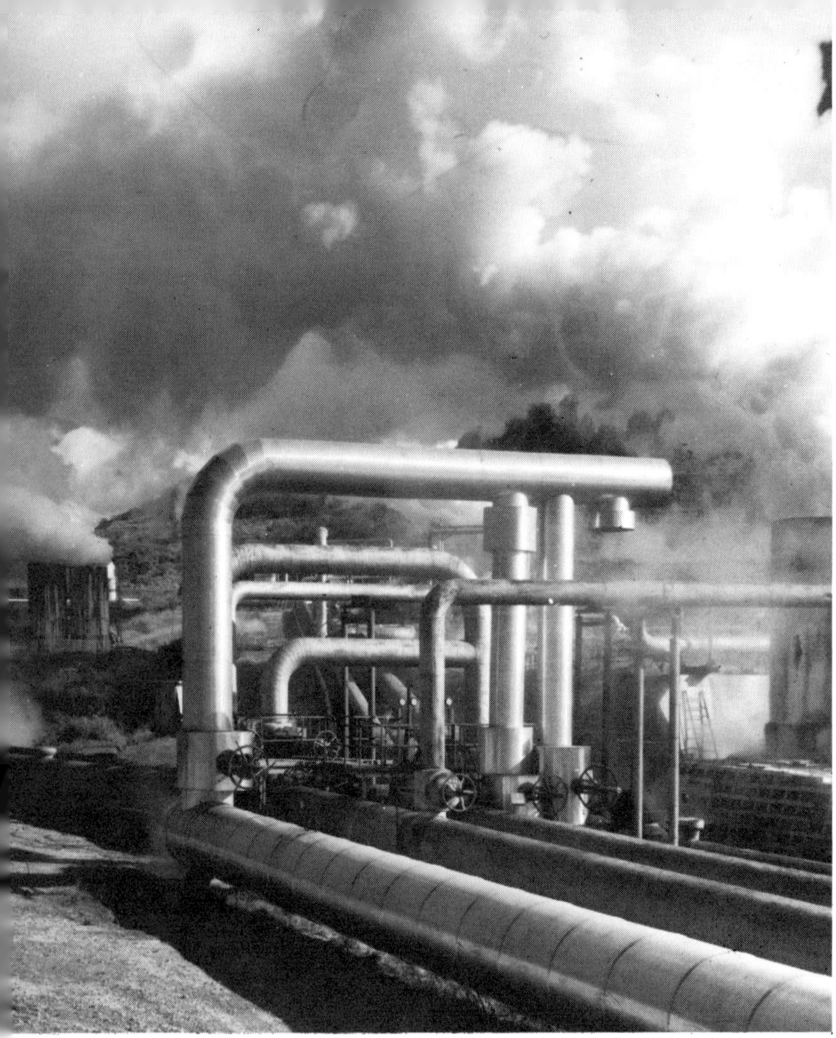

Above *The steam pipeline and steam boreholes at the Wairakei Geothermal field in New Zealand.*

geothermal energy

The earth's heat can be used to make electricity and heat buildings. In fifteen countries, e.g. New Zealand, Japan, the USSR, USA and Italy, this has been done for many years. The natural hot water

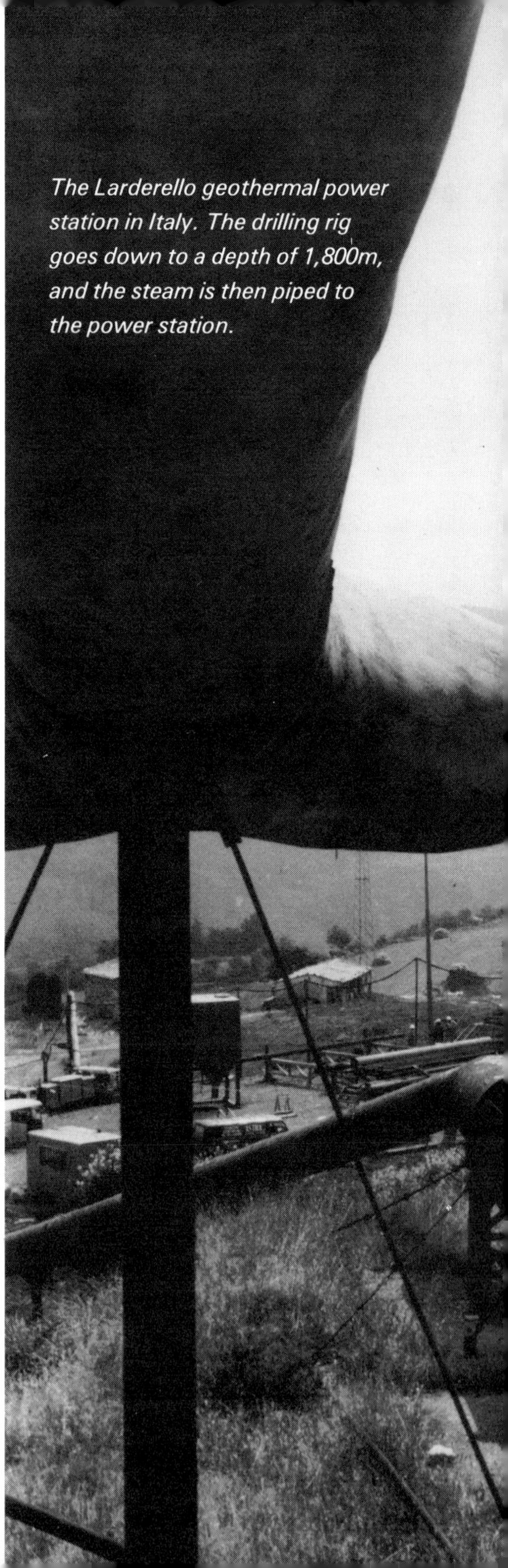

The Larderello geothermal power station in Italy. The drilling rig goes down to a depth of 1,800m, and the steam is then piped to the power station.

reservoirs underground are like pressure cookers. When well are sunk into them steam hisses out. This steam can be used in a power house to make electricity. The steam of the Lardarello field in Italy has been driving turbines for electricity since 1904. The fields may produce steam or hot water, or they may consist of hot rock underground. The hot water field is the most usual.

One problem is that the land above the reservoirs can sink when the water is removed. Some wells give off the poisonous gas hydrogen sulphide with its "bad eggs" smell. Also the water can contain large quantities of dissolved solids, such as salt.

At about 4,000 km (2,300 miles) underground the temperature is about 300 degrees Centigrade. How can we use this heat? One way would be to force water underground and then pump it, once heated, back to the surface.

Geothermal energy could become a great energy source in the years ahead. Some people predict that in fifty years from now geothermal energy will be more important than oil.

fuel cells

Fuel cells have been widely used in space. They are too expensive for large-scale use on earth. Hydrogen, natural gas or a liquid like methyl alcohol is pumped or poured into the cell—a sort of battery—and electricity is generated.

Below *This fuel cell power unit can generate up to 5kW of electricity. It is small enough to go in a van. It uses a cheap liquid fuel and air.*

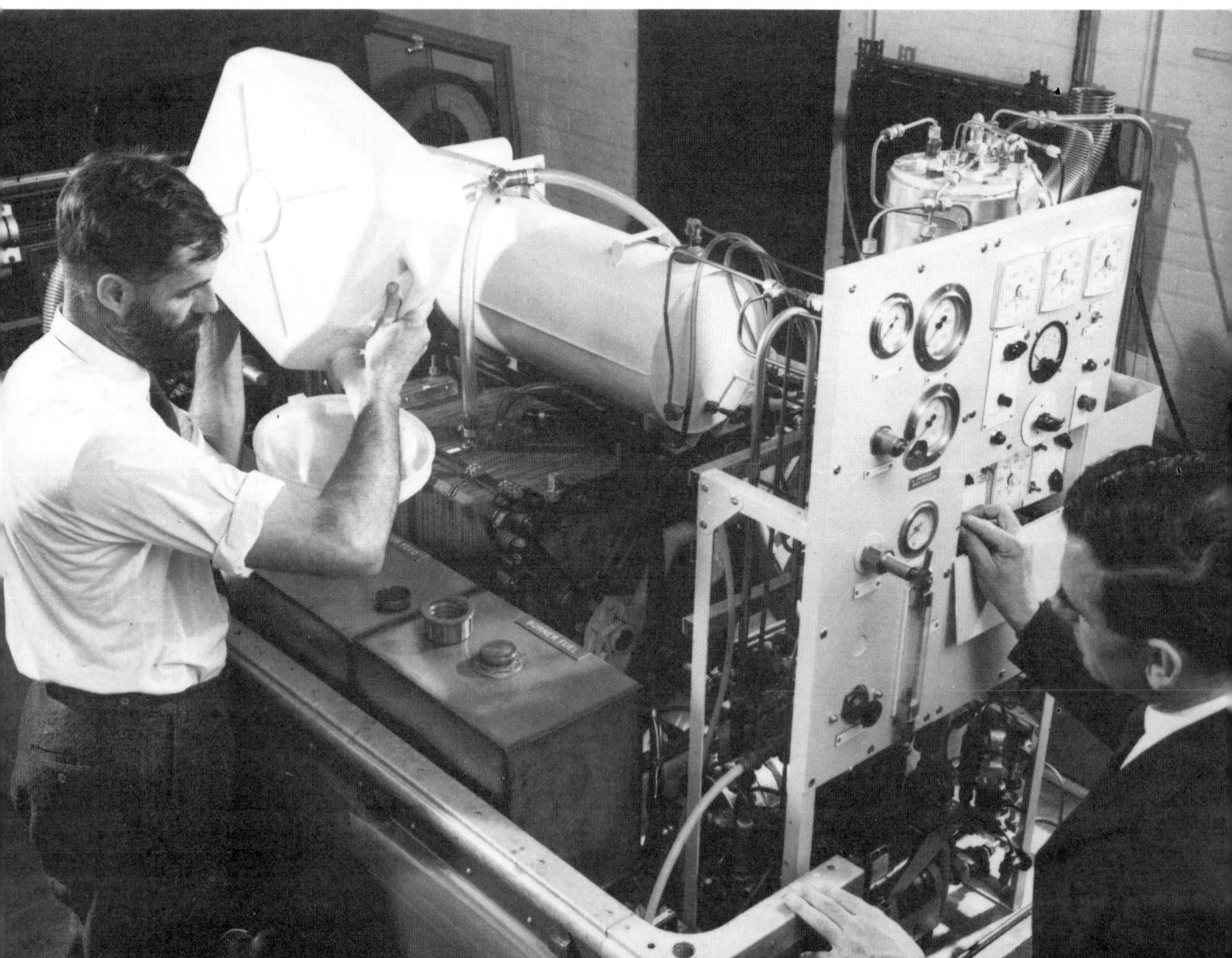

the winds and tides

The movement of the air and the sea are attractive energy sources. They are free, and using them does not cause pollution.

There are only a few sites suitable for harnessing tidal energy. These places are on estuaries, like that at Rance in France. Electricity is generated from the ebb and flow of the sea. There have long been plans to put a barrage system in the Severn Estuary in the UK. Most countries with a coastline could use tidal power to generate some electricity.

Left, above *A 5kW electro wind generator.*

Left, below *This "Winco" produces 200W of electricity.*

It is hard to make a windmill which will cope with the wind in all weathers. The wind changes strength, and it also changes direction. To make all a country's energy, too many huge windmills would be needed. They would have to be put in pretty, hilly sites, too. But this is a useful source for remote and less developed areas.

67

oil shales and tar sands

There are very large deposits of oil which cannot be taken by sinking wells. *Tar sand* is a sandstone containing tarry oil. Over 90% of known deposits are divided equally between Canada and Venezuela. Most of the rest is in the USA. Geologists think that we could take 1,500,000 million barrels of oil from the deposits. There are many difficulties to be solved. An enormous amount of rock, earth and sand has to be removed. For every 100,000 barrels of oil, 100 million tons of rock has to be moved. Is it worth the effort?

Oil shales are different. The oil there is not liquid, but solid. It is called kerogen. At about 370 degrees Centigrade this changes into a light shale oil. There are about 6,850,000 million barrels worth. Major deposits are found in Brazil and Utah, USA. The Canadian tar sands could produce 1.25 million barrels of oil a day by 1985. Shale oil production could be 400,000 barrels a day in the USA by 1985.

At present, it costs less to produce shale oil than oil from coal. This could easily change with all the research into coal.

The Athabasca oil sands in Canada are one of the world's greatest deposits of oil. For years oilmen had tried to extract the oil, and failed. Now at last the oil is in production.

9 Protecting the environment

Left *This new freeway in Durban, South Africa speeds traffic through the city. Is it wise to let the motor car take up so much space, and cause so much pollution?*

Nearly all the ways we produce energy change the environment or harm it in some way. Dirt and poisonous gases fill the air. Oil and chemicals pollute the rivers and the sea. Landscapes are scarred or disfigured.

Pembroke Power Station, Wales. This station burns oil from the Milford Haven refineries and has an output of 2,000 MW of electricity. This kind of station produces pollution in the air.

People today know how easy it is to spoil the environment and how difficult it is to restore it. There are laws limiting the amount of substances released into the environment—but still we continue to pollute.

The main pollutants are:
— sulphur dioxide (this gas is formed from the sulphur impurities in coal and oil when they are burned. It can combine with oxygen and water to form sulphuric acid, a corrosive liquid)
— nitrogen oxides (poisonous gases)
— carbon monoxide (a poisonous gas)
— lead (a poisonous metal that accumulates in the body)
— hydrocarbons (can produce cancer)

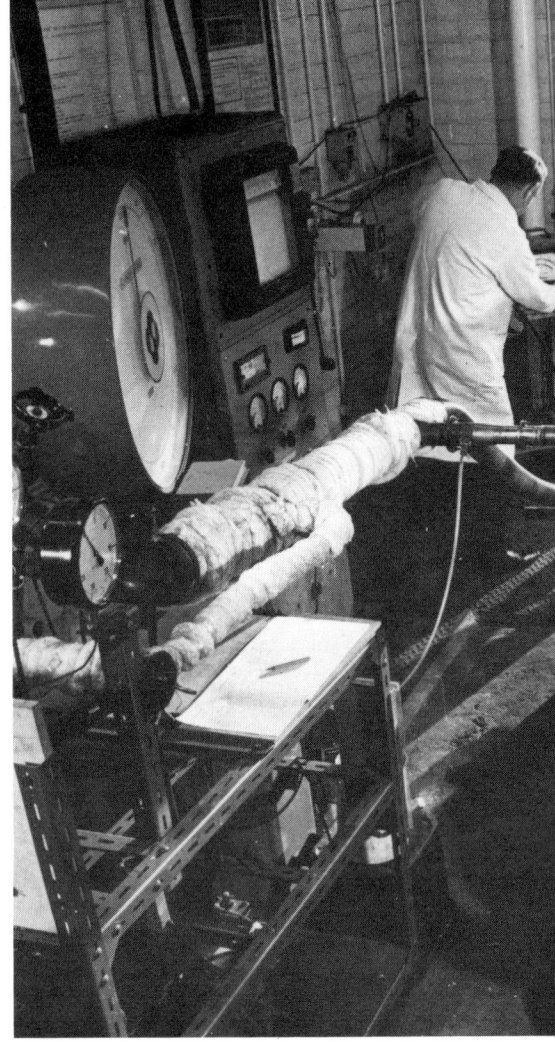

Left *These turbines in Battersea power station supply heat to a housing estate and a block of flats. This is one way that waste heat from power stations can be well used.*

Above *Tests being carried out at the Thornton Research Centre in England on the petrol (gasoline) engine. Changes can be made to the ordinary car engine which make it less polluting.*

Above right *The flask being lifted is a special design to hold spent fuel from a nuclear reactor. It is going to Windscale reprocessing plant.*

— particulates, specks of solids (can produce breathing problems)
— radioactive material, from the nuclear power industry (causes cancer)
— heat pollution, from power stations (disturbs the balance of life in rivers or sea)
— carbon dioxide, formed when coal, oil, or natural gas is burned (not poisonous, but can change our weather)

We cannot yet remove sulphur dioxide from the chimney gases of power stations. Very tall chimneys are often used to disperse the gas. Oil and coal without sulphur impurities are rare and therefore expensive.

Above *The multi-flue chimney at this coal-fired power station at Ratcliffe, England has a multi-flue chimney 115m tall. This helps disperse the polluting discharge, but the chemicals come down eventually.*

Above right *This picture was taken in 1940, before anti-pollution laws, in Pittsburgh, USA.*

Cars cause pollution, particularly in crowded cities. Laws in the USA keep strict control of exhaust gases. The "smogs" (smoke + fog) of twenty years ago have gone thanks to laws preventing burning of coal in open grates. Still our ancient buildings are being ruined, and roadside plants are poisonous. Oil spills at sea suffocate and kill fish and birds. The detergents used to clean it up are just as harmful to life in the sea. Most oil pollution comes from the washing of empty tanks at sea rather than from accidents.

This ship carries equipment for coping with oil spills. Sand is treated with chemicals so that oil clings to the individual grains. The sand, and the oil, sink to the bottom.

75

Large power stations use an enormous amount of water for cooling. This water goes into the nearby river, estuary or lake— and raises its temperature. This disturbs the natural balance of plant and animal life in the water. Fish can grow faster in the warmer water, but it would be better if we could use the warm water for heating buildings. Often this is impossible because power stations are built so far away from where people live. Modern power stations with their large cooling towers and tall chimneys are difficult to hide. Open-cast mining can badly scar the landscape, but if money is spent the land can be restored.

Above *A flask of used fuel is about to be reprocessed at Windscale.*

Unlike the power station in Battersea, this one in Pembroke, South Wales, is too far from home to supply useful heat.

Above right *The new reprocessing plant at Windscale. Every safety precaution is taken, but many still think that the risks involved with nuclear power are too great.*

The most dangerous power source is nuclear energy. Radioactive materials must be handled with particular care. Some say they should not be produced at all. They could make the earth dangerous for thousands of years.

Protecting the environment requires constant care and attention. Laws are needed to force us not to pollute. All pollution control costs money, and we have to decide how clean an environment we are willing to pay for.

10 Using fuel well

CLOSE WINDOWS
keep warmth in

When fuel was cheap we wasted a lot. We never should have and now we cannot afford to. At home, in travel, in school, at the office and in the factory we need to "save it". How?

1 By using less. For example, we can have lower room temperatures, and use different means of transport.
2 By using energy more efficiently. We can have better machinery in better condition. This way we get the same job done with less energy.

CLOSE DOORS
keep warmth in

turn off unwanted lights

SAVE IT

Energy sense is common sense.

at home

There are two energy watchwords to remember at home:

INSULATE and REGULATE

Insulation is very poor in many older houses. Most of the heat is lost through the floors, the roof, the windows, walls and doors. With no insulation, we lose 25% of the money spent on fuel. Some remedies are quite cheap. Check the insulation in your home against this list:

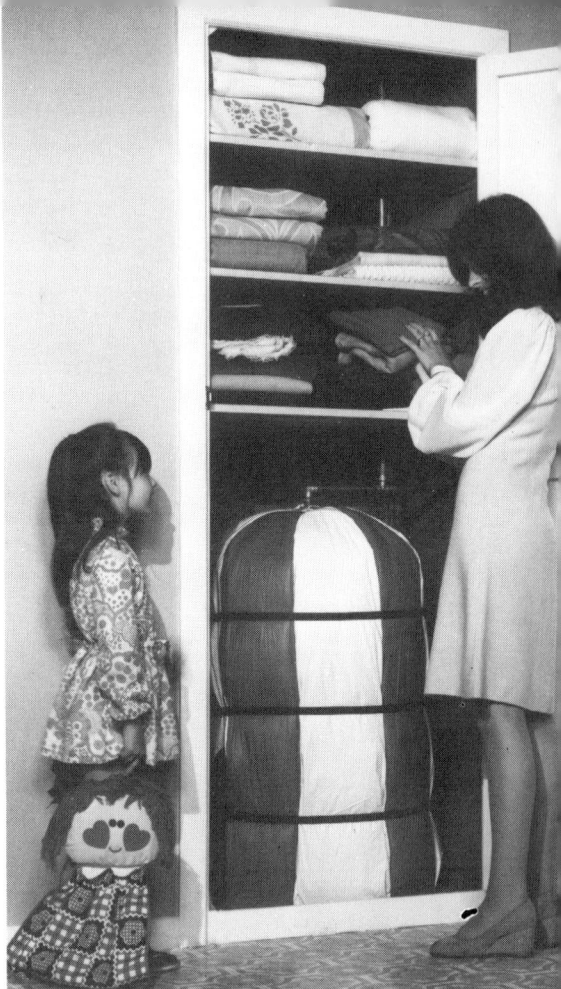

1 Is the loft insulated? There should be at least 7cm (3in) "fibreglass" or mica chips.
2 Is the hot water tank insulated? It should have a 7cm (3in) jacket to keep it warm.
3 Are all outside hot water pipes lagged?
4 Are the outside doors a good fit?
5 Is the floor covered with a fitted carpet and underlay? If there is no carpet, or if it is not fitted, have all the holes and gaps been filled in?

Above *Mineral fibre slabs built into new cavity walls.*

Left *A 7cm jacket round the water heater saves its cost in a few weeks.*

Below *Loft insulation saves heat normally lost through the roof.*

6 If the house has cavity walls (walls with two "skins" of brick and an air gap between) are they filled with plastic foam or mineral wool?

7 Are the windows double-glazed?

If you can answer "yes" to all these questions, then your home is top of the insulation league. Many of you will find that you answer "no" to nearly all. Here is what you can do. Points 1-5 are not very expensive jobs, and they are effective. Fitted carpets are best but expensive; filling holes is cheap and effective. It should be done even if a carpet is going to be fitted. Points 6 and 7 are more costly. They are worthwhile, but may take a few years to repay the cost.

in travel

Walking and cycling are healthier and cheaper than cars. Public transport saves fuel compared to cars. Also, if there are many people in one vehicle, that means there is less traffic and fewer hold-ups. If you have to use a car, see if you can give someone a lift.

in school and the office

The same points about insulation apply here as at home. Because there are more people in the building, the "switch off" watchword has to be applied more carefully. Also the type of lighting used is more important. The fluorescent tube is four times more efficient than the ordinary glowing filament bulb.

Make sure the windows are not left open unnecessarily. Switch off lights when they are not needed, and keep doors closed. Keep furniture, curtains and clothing (coats, etc) well clear of radiators, so that the hot air can circulate freely.

in the factory

The rules we have already learned apply to factories. They also have machinery and furnaces which use vast amounts of energy. Economy is very important. About 10% of the energy being used could be saved with a little spending and by good economy. We could save more by having efficient machinery. This can cost a lot of money to install, but could make great savings in the long term.

In order to provide tomorrow's generations with energy, we must save it today.

Finding out more

Large oil and gas companies usually have information departments or education services. They provide booklets, wallcharts, filmstrips, audio-cassettes, cut-out models and so on. Sometimes visits to installations can be arranged. You can write to

The Institute of Petroleum Information Service, 61 New Cavendish Street, London W1.

Schools Information Centre on the Chemical Industry, The Polytechnic of North London, Holloway Road, London N7.

Books to read

Energy Today by John A G Thomas, published by Kay & Ward.

World Resources of Energy and *Conserving the Earth's Resources,* two titles in the World Topics series published by Macdonald Educational.

Fuel and Power in the Macdonald Junior Reference Library.

Oil, Gas and *Coal* in the Men and Materials series published by Macmillan Education.

Oil by Roger Vielvoye, Jackdaw No 141.

Glossary

COALPLEX A possible coal "refinery" of the future in which oil, gas, chemicals and electricity will be produced from coal.

CONTROLLED CHAIN REACTION See NUCLEAR CHAIN REACTION.

DEEP MINING See MINING.

EARTH'S CRUST The top layer of the earth consisting of rocks. Its average depth is not more than 65 kilometres.

FAST BREEDER REACTION See NUCLEAR REACTORS.

FOSSIL FUELS Remains of organisms embedded in the surface of the earth with high carbon and/or hydrogen content. The main ones are coal, oil and natural gas.

GEOTHERMAL ENERGY Heat stored below the earth's surface, which can be in the form of hot water, steam or hot rocks.

HYDRO-ELECTRICITY Electricity generated from the energy in falling water.

LIQUEFIED NATURAL GAS (LNG) Natural gas is a liquid at high pressures. It is cheaper to transport it in this form over long distances in special ships.

MINING Coal can occur near the surface or deep underground. When it is near the surface it can be removed using giant scoops. This is called open-cast mining (or in the USA strip-mining). Deep mining has to be undertaken when coal is deep underground. Shafts are sunk and tunnels built supported by automatic pit props which advance as the coal is cut.

NATURAL GAS Mainly the gas methane, CH_4. It is a fossil fuel which occurs with oil and sometimes alone.

NUCLEAR CHAIN REACTION A continuing nuclear fission reaction in which neutrons from split atomic nuclei split other nuclei. A controlled chain reaction takes place in a nuclear reactor. An uncontrolled chain reaction takes place in the atomic bomb.

NUCLEAR FISSION Splitting of a nucleus of a heavy atom (e.g. uranium) into two lighter fragments plus free neutrons. A lot of energy is released.

NUCLEAR FUEL Usually means the fuel for nuclear fission reactors—uranium or plutonium.

NUCLEAR FUSION The combining of two light atoms (e.g. hydrogen or deuterium) releasing even more energy than fission.

NUCLEAR REACTORS Devices in which controlled nuclear chain reactions take place to produce heat. The fast breeder reactor is a highly efficient reactor which can produce (breed) more fuel than it consumes.

OIL SHALES A solid called kerogen which decomposes at about 370 degrees Centigrade to give a light shale oil.

PHOTOSYNTHESIS A complicated process in green plants whereby water and carbon are absorbed from the air and converted into glucose. Chlorophyll—which gives the plants their green colour—is essential to this process.

PUMPED WATER STORAGE Two water reservoirs at different heights on a mountain side. At times of low demand for electricity water is pumped from the bottom to the top reservoirs. At times of peak demand water is allowed to rush from the top to the bottom turning a turbo-generator to produce electricity.

REFINERY A highly complex chemical factory in which crude oil (from the oil well) is boiled and condensed (distilled) to give a wide range of products, e.g. petrol (gasoline) for cars, heating oil for oil burners.

SOLAR CELLS See SOLAR ENERGY.

SOLAR ENERGY The energy of the sun. It can be collected by solar panels and used for heating buildings. Or, using a solar cell, it can be converted directly into electricity.

SOLAR HEATING See SOLAR ENERGY.

TAR SANDS Porous sandstone containing oil.

WAVE POWER The natural movement of the waves and tides which can be harnessed to produce electricity.

Index

Picture Credits

The author and publishers would like to thank those who gave permission for their pictures to be reproduced on the following pages:
American Gas Association, 40; BP, 8, 34; Central Electricity Generating Board, 42, 43, 44, 45, 46, 47, 48 (both), 49, 71, 72 (below), 74, 76; The Electricity Council, 6, 10, 13 (both), 14; National Coal Board, Frontispiece, 11, 25, 26, 27, 28, 31; Natural Energy Company, 67 (both), New Zealand Embassy, 64; Science Museum, 12; Shell, 6, 12, 14, 15, 17, 22, 33, 35, 36, 37, 38, 66, 69, 70, 72 (above), 75 (below); United Kingdom Atomic Energy Authority, 17, 51 (both), 52, 53 (both), 55 (both), 56, 57, 62, 63, 73, 77 (both); United Nations, 59, 65; Wayland Picture Library, 8, 9, 30; World Health Organisation, 75 (top).